LEVEL
3

T0206571

Robots

Melissa Stewart

NATIONAL
GEOGRAPHIC

Washington, D.C.

For Bruce, who loves his Roomba —M. S.

The author and publisher gratefully acknowledge the expert review of this book by Natanel Dukan of Aldebaran Robotics.

Published by National Geographic Partners, LLC, Washington, DC 20036.

Book design by YAY! Design

Trade paperback ISBN: 978-1-4263-1344-8
Reinforced library binding ISBN: 978-1-4263-1345-5

Printed in the United States of America
22/WOR/10

Table of Contents

What's a Robot?

What do you think of when you hear the word ROBOT? A blinking, walking, robo-talking metal person? Some robots really do look like people, but most don't.

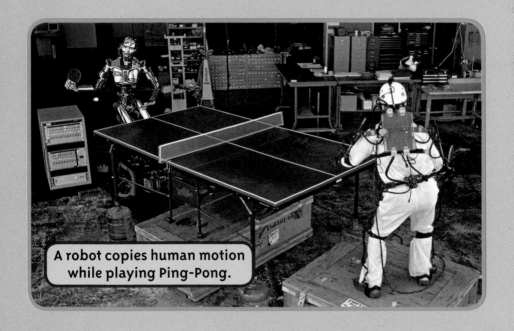

A robot copies human motion while playing Ping-Pong.

Robots come in almost every shape, size, and color you can think of. They can look like fish or flies, lobsters or spiders. Some look like nothing else you've ever seen.

A scientist gives Sojourner, a robotic rover, one last check before its mission to Mars.

A robot, or bot, is a machine that has movable parts and can make decisions. People design it to do a job by itself.

How is a robot like a person? It collects information from its surroundings.

A robot in Japan steers traffic away from highway construction.

Then it processes the information and figures out the best way to do its job.

But a robot doesn't think the way a person does. It can only do things that engineers and roboticists (roh-BOT-ti-sists) program into its computer "brain."

Tech Talk

PROGRAM: To give a set of instructions to a machine

ROBOTICIST: A person who builds robots

SURROUNDINGS: The conditions and things around a person or object

Researchers built the first robots about fifty years ago. But people had been thinking about mechanical "humans" for a long, long time.

850 B.C.	A.D. 1495	1961	1970
Ancient Greek poet Homer described bot-like creatures that did anything their masters asked.	Italian artist and scientist Leonardo da Vinci drew plans for a mechanical man in his notebooks.	The world's first robot went to work assembling cars at a General Motors plant in Ewing, New Jersey, U.S.A.	Roboticists in Stanford, California, U.S.A., built the first robot that could move and sense its surroundings.

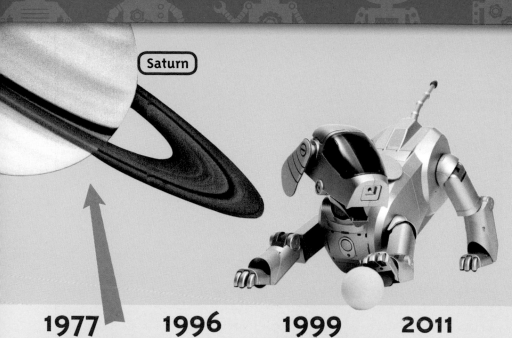

Saturn

1977

The Voyager 1 and 2 space probes were launched to study Saturn, Jupiter, and their many moons.

1996

Researchers at Honda introduced P2, the first human-like robot.

1999

Sony developed AIBO, a robotic dog that could interact with people.

2011

R2 was launched to the International Space Station, making it the first human-like robot in space.

Every robot is designed for a specific job. And that job determines what the robot looks like. But no matter what a robot does, it has three kinds of parts—a computer, sensors, and actuators.

A robot's computer is like a person's brain. It uses the instructions programmed by a roboticist to make decisions. The sensors are like a person's eyes, ears, nose, and skin. They collect information about the robot's surroundings and send messages to the computer. A robot's actuators receive messages from the computer. They control the robot's movements, lights, speaking, and more.

Tech Talk

SENSOR: A robot part that detects light, temperature, pressure, sound, or motion

ACTUATOR: A robot part that performs an action

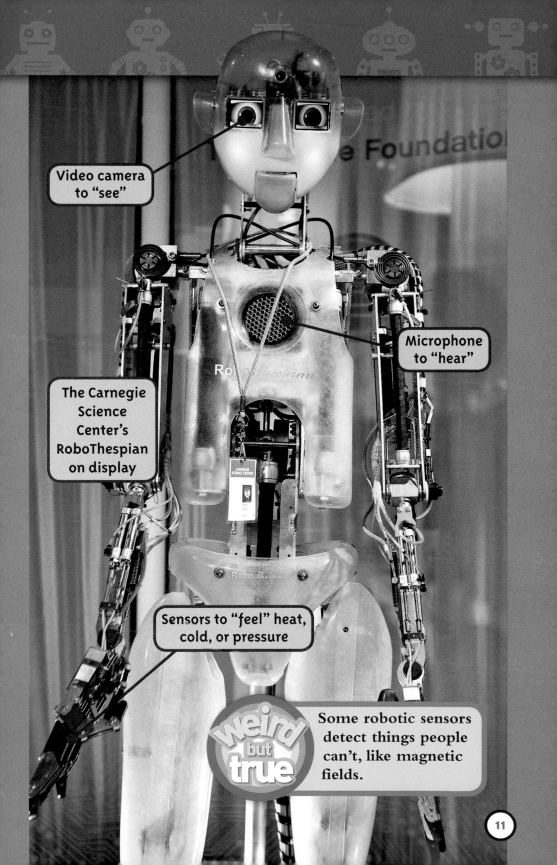

Video camera to "see"

Microphone to "hear"

The Carnegie Science Center's RoboThespian on display

Sensors to "feel" heat, cold, or pressure

weird but true

Some robotic sensors detect things people can't, like magnetic fields.

7 Cool Robots

Robots can do lots of interesting things. Which of these awesome robots would you like to have?

1 Each year, NAO (Now) bots compete in an international robot soccer match. Researchers make improvements after watching the robots play.

2

3

RoboLobster may one day search the ocean floor for mines and sunken ships.

4 RIBA was designed to lift patients from a bed or the floor.

5 Lean and light, HRP-4 can stand on one leg. It also responds to voice commands.

6 In China, robotic waiters zip around restaurants delivering meals.

7 RoboTuna swims to explore deep ocean areas and coral reefs.

Go Bots!

All robots have movable parts, but only some can travel from place to place. That's because it's difficult and expensive to build bots that can go, go, go.

Robots that weld car parts and inspect food containers don't need to move across factory floors. But when a bot has to get around, roboticists choose one of three systems—tracks, wheels, or legs.

Tracks

Robots with tracks are rugged and reliable. They are perfect for moving across uneven ground, but they move slowly. Engineers design them to disarm bombs, fight fires, and travel in space.

This robot disarms bombs for the U.S. Marine Corps. It moves around on tracks to do its job.

track

track

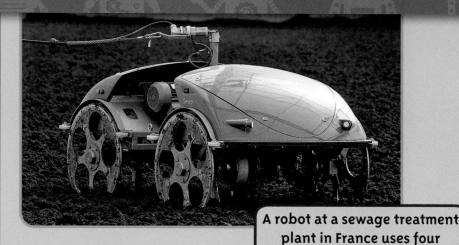

A robot at a sewage treatment plant in France uses four wheels and solar energy.

Wheels

Robots with wheels are fast, but they may tip over on bumpy ground. Roboticists build them to mow lawns, guard prisons, patrol buildings at night, and carry materials inside factories and hospitals.

Legs

Robots with legs can step over objects or climb up walls. They are perfect for cleaning up chemical spills or exploring uneven areas of the ocean floor.

This four-legged robot was designed to explore the site of a nuclear accident in Japan. It can release a smaller robot that fits into small spaces.

Nature Knows Best

Roboticists also study animals for ideas about motion. Borrowing ideas from nature is a science called biomimetics (BYE-oh-mih-MET-iks).

These little ladybug robots move just like the insects they are named after.

Tech Talk

BIOMIMETICS: Copying the shape and movement of animals in a machine's design

This robot moves and climbs just like a gecko lizard. That makes it perfect for searching for injured people after tornadoes or earthquakes.

Animals are really good at moving around on this planet. They hop across rocky cliffs. They slither and scuttle over sand. They fly and swim and tunnel underground. Many motions that animals use can also be used by robots.

LS3 is being designed for the U.S. Army to carry heavy packs for soldiers.

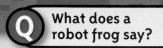
The LS3 robot has legs that work like a dog's. It can follow a person and move safely around trees and rocks. Engineers hope that one day the robot will follow spoken commands like a loyal dog.

A robot named Cyro moves through the water just like a jellyfish. The U.S. Navy plans to use the beach-umbrella-size bot to keep watch over coastal waters. Cyro could also make maps of the ocean floor and study sea life.

A thick layer of a squishy material called silicone gives Cyro a body that looks like a real jellyfish.

Imagine a robotic snake coming to life by remote control. As the robot wriggles from side to side like a python, its mechanical body slowly inches forward. Tiny cameras line the bot's long body, so you can see what the robot snake sees.

A real tiger python

This snake could help with rescues in natural disasters. Snakes are the perfect shape to navigate through collapsed buildings after an earthquake. They can go where people can't.

Tech Talk

NAVIGATE: To locate a place and plan a path to get there

Robot snakes, called snakebots, can climb trees and swim, too.

weird but true

Doctors use tiny snakebots during some surgeries because they can curve around body organs.

Robots at Work

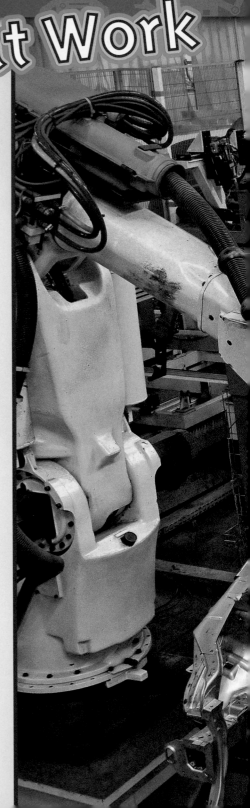

Most robots do jobs that people can't do or don't want to do. Name a repetitive or dangerous job. Somewhere, a robot is probably doing it.

Robots control some city trains at night, so human workers can get a good night's sleep. Factory robots arrange chocolates in boxes, spray-paint cars, build computers, and perform many other jobs.

Car companies depend on robotic arms to do dozens of jobs. These factory robots are welding together metal parts.

Robots have no trouble working in blistering heat, freezing cold, or places that smell bad. They can explore active volcanoes, visit distant planets, and spend days tracking enemy soldiers in the desert.

This computer art shows the ACTUV robot ship that is designed to track enemy submarines for up to 90 days at sea.

This photo of the eight-legged robot Dante II was taken just before it went down into an active volcano in Alaska.

Robots are useful workers because they don't take vacations or stop to eat lunch. All they need to do their job is power from an electric outlet or a battery.

Robots at Home

You don't need to push or turn this lawnmower. It senses when it has reached the edge of your lawn and turns itself.

Nobody likes mowing the lawn, so roboticists invented a bot to do the job. It senses an invisible fence, so it doesn't leave the yard.

weird but true

In Tokyo, you can buy a piano-playing robot for $42,000!

Nobody likes to do housework, either. So now there are robots that can vacuum your rugs. When a vacuum bot senses a wall, it backs up and rolls in a new direction.

There is also a robot alarm clock on wheels. If you don't get up, the bot jumps off your nightstand and rolls around your room. You have to get up to turn it off.

Robot alarm clock

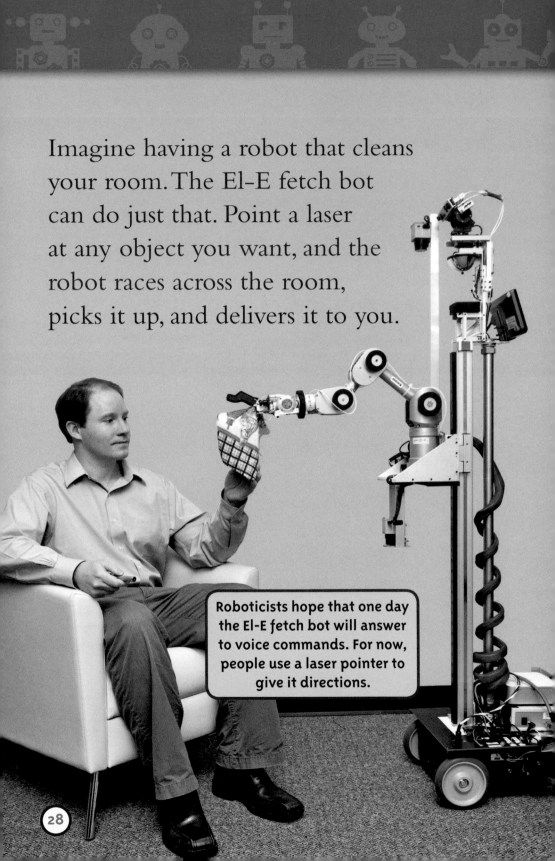

Imagine having a robot that cleans your room. The El-E fetch bot can do just that. Point a laser at any object you want, and the robot races across the room, picks it up, and delivers it to you.

Roboticists hope that one day the El-E fetch bot will answer to voice commands. For now, people use a laser pointer to give it directions.

Yurina can be controlled by a touch screen, a joystick, or voice commands.

Researchers designed the El-E fetch bot to help people who have trouble getting around, but one day it could be in homes all over the world.

Roboticists are also hard at work on Yurina. It is designed to help people who are sick or disabled take a bath or move from a chair to a bed.

Pushing the Limits!

What did robotocist Kogoro Kurata have in mind when he set out to build the world's biggest bot? He just wanted to see if he could. Kurata is like a lot of roboticists. They try new things just to see if they're possible.

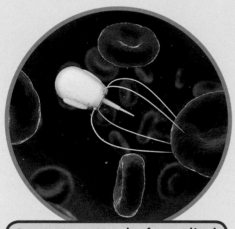

Computer artwork of a medical nanobot in the bloodstream

Other roboticists are working on bots so small they could swim through a person's blood. One day, these nanobots might be able to attack cancer cells or carry medicine to just one part of the body.

 **Tech Talk**

NANOBOT: A robot so small you need a microscope to see it

Kurata's robot is the biggest robot ever made. You have to climb high to sit in the control seat of this 13-foot-tall robot.

Almost Human

Researchers at Honda have been building robots that look and act like humans for more than 15 years. The latest version is called ASIMO. It can dance, balance on one leg, and even climb stairs. It can pick up objects, speak to people, and recognize faces and voices. Wow!

weird but true

There's an ASIMO action figure sold in Japan.

Schoolchildren in Tokyo, Japan, answer questions from their android teacher, Saya.

Androids are lifelike robots. Everything about them is artificial, but sometimes it's hard to tell they aren't real. Some androids seem to blink, breathe, twitch, and talk just like a real person.

Tech Talk

ANDROID: A robot that looks or acts like a person

ARTIFICIAL: Made by humans

A roboticist named Cynthia Breazeal taught her robot Kismet about feelings. When she started, Kismet was just like a baby. She programmed it to like brightly colored toys and people and to want to rest at times. She gave it sixteen computers and many cameras—sensors for sight.

Roboticist Cynthia Breazeal works with Kismet. It reacts to what she does.

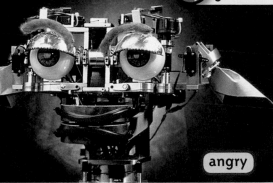
angry

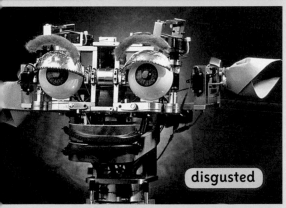
disgusted

Kismet can make different faces to show emotions.

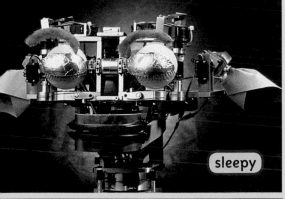
sleepy

Then she invited kids and grown-ups to come play with Kismet. When Kismet's cameras saw a happy, smiling face, Kismet learned to react in a very human way—by smiling back!

happy

Real Robots or Movie Magic?

Real robots can't move or speak as well as the robot characters you see in movies like *Star Wars* or *WALL-E*. What you see on the screen is the result of movie magic.

Can you name these movie robots? (Answers are on page 37.)

1

2

3

4

5

WALL·E

Robots in Space

Robots can explore places that humans can't go. Humans have traveled to the moon, but robots have landed on Mars, and they've collected information while circling Venus and Jupiter. Robots have also traveled to the edge of our solar system and even beyond it.

In 1977, scientists launched two Voyager spacecraft into space. These spacecraft have traveled more than 11 billion miles and are still sending information back to Earth.

An illustration of Voyager 1, a spacecraft built by NASA engineers to photograph and study Jupiter, Saturn, and their moons

R2 can grasp handheld tools and lift up to 40 pounds. It doesn't need to sleep or eat or go to the bathroom like people do.

R2 has been aboard the International Space Station since 2011. The human-like robonaut uses camera sensors in its head to see. R2's computer is in its belly. One day, robonauts may work side by side with human astronauts.

Tech Talk
ROBONAUT: A robot astronaut

Two rover robots are exploring Mars.
Opportunity has been cruising around
the red planet since 2004. Curiosity
landed in 2012.

Computer art
of Opportunity

Computer art
of Curiosity

Both bots are studying the planet's air, soil, and rocks. Scientists are looking for signs of ancient life on Mars. They also want to know how much of the planet was once covered with water.

Armed and Ready

Curiosity's seven-foot-long robotic arm is loaded with tools. Its wire brush clears away Martian dust. Its hammer drill pulls rock samples from below the surface.

Scientists designed Curiosity for a two-year mission, but they hope it will continue to send back information for even longer.

You Can Build Bots

Think you'd like to build a bot? You aren't alone. Each year, more than 200,000 kids ages 9 to 16 join *FIRST*® LEGO® League (FLL®). They work on teams that research and solve a science question or problem. Then they build and program LEGO® robots to do a series of jobs.

After about ten weeks of planning, building, and programming, many FLL® teams get together at big events where they can win awards and prizes.

Sound like fun? Let your parents and teachers know. They can help you start an FLL® team at your school.

Robots of the Future

It will be a long time before a household bot does all your cooking and cleaning. But in just a few years, a robot might drive you to school.

Right now several companies are developing robotic cars that drive themselves. Covered with sensors, robo-cars are safer and use less gas than the cars we drive today.

What other amazing robo-inventions will soon be part of our lives? We'll just have to wait and see.

This robotic car is taking pictures and mapping streets in Brasilia, Brazil.

Glossary

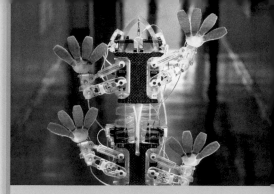

ACTUATOR: A robot part that performs an action

BIOMIMETICS: Copying the shape and movement of animals in a machine's design

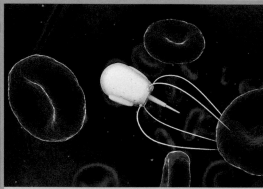

NANOBOT: A robot so small you need a microscope to see it

ROBONAUT: A robot astronaut

ROBOTICIST: A person who builds robots

ANDROID: A robot that looks or acts like a person

ARTIFICIAL: Made by humans

NAVIGATE: To locate a place and plan a path to get there

PROGRAM: To give a set of instructions to a machine

SENSOR: A robot part that detects light, temperature, pressure, sound, or motion

SURROUNDINGS: The conditions and things around a person or object

Index

Illustration are
indicated by
boldface.